LANDSCAPES of LEGEND

BENEATH THE EARTH

— ✦ The facts and the fables ✦ —

Finn Bevan
Illustrated by Diana Mayo

W
FRANKLIN WATTS
NEW YORK • LONDON • SYDNEY

First published in 1998 by Franklin Watts
96 Leonard Street, London EC2A 4RH

Franklin Watts Australia
14 Mars Road
Lane Cove
NSW 2066

Text © Finn Bevan 1998
Illustrations © Diana Mayo 1998

Series editor: Rachel Cooke
Art director: Robert Walster
Designer: Mo Choy
Picture research: Sue Mennell

A CIP catalogue record for this book
is available from the British Library.

ISBN 0 7496 2956 8

Dewey Classification 398.2

Printed in Singapore

Picture acknowledgements:
AKG London p. 11 (Erich Lessing); Axiom Photographic Agency p. 18 (Jim Holmes);
C.M. Dixon p. 10; Werner Forman Archive pp. 6, 15 (British Museum, London);
Hutchison Library p. 24b; Planet Earth Pictures pp. 14 (Krafft), 24t (Ken Lucas);
Slide File p. 20.

Contents

Mysteries of the Earth   4

Into the Underworld   6
The goddess and the pomegranate   7
A Roman myth of Proserpina, queen of the Underworld

Secret Caves   10
The birth of Zeus   12
A Greek myth of the secret birth of Zeus, king of the gods

Fountains of Fire   14
How Pele found a home   16
A Hawaiian story of the volcano goddess, Pele

The Shaking Earth   18
How a giant catfish shook the world   19
A Japanese story that explains how earthquakes happen

Springs of Life   20
Finn and the Salmon of Knowledge   22
An Irish tale of the great hero, Finn MacCool

Riches from the Earth   24
Andvari's gold   26
A Viking tale of the theft of gold from Andvari the Dwarf

Notes and Explanations   30

Index   32

Mysteries of the Earth

Ancient people could only guess what lay beneath their feet. They knew about caves, which led them to believe that the Earth was hollow, criss-crossed by a maze of underground passages – a cold, dark world. Others knew about volcanoes, and thought it must be extremely hot underground. But no one knew for certain, so myths and legends grew up to explain the distant, shadowy regions beneath the Earth.

Worlds Underground

Many people believed that the Underworld lay underground: a deep, dark place to which people's souls travelled after death. Like everything else, the Underworld was controlled by the gods. There were many different versions of what the Underworld looked like.

In African legend, the Earth was divided into two parts, separated by an ocean. Above was the land of the living, rising up like a high mountain. Below the ocean lay the Underworld, which was almost identical, with houses, rivers and hills, but facing downwards. In this upside-down version of the land of the living, people slept by day and came out at night.

Although the gloomy regions beneath the Earth were believed to be places of the dead, where their souls wandered for eternity, they were also a source of life and wealth. The soil nourished the crops and plants on which people's lives depended. From the rocks of the Earth came gold and precious stones, so valuable that they were often seen as gifts from the gods.

Thankful for these gifts, people often saw the Earth as a place of creation. Many myths tell how people were made from mud and clay, while the Incas of Peru believed that their ancestors came from beneath the Earth. These were three brothers and three sisters, who appeared through three sacred caves near the city of Cuzco. They were dressed in the finest woollen clothes and wore earrings of purest gold to show their royal status.

Into the Underworld

In the myths of Ancient Greece and Rome, the Underworld (Hades) was the place of the dead. The Roman poet Virgil wrote that the entrance to the Underworld lay deep beneath Lake Avernus, near Naples, Italy. The lake's landscape is volcanic, with pools of mud bubbling from the ground and an eerie stink of sulphur.

Telling the Future

Near Lake Avernus, the hillside is pitted with caves believed to lead to Hades. The most famous is the Cave of the Cumaean Sibyl, an ancient Greek prophetess, who gave advice and told the future. It was the Sibyl who lead Aeneas, the legendary Roman hero, to the kingdom of the dead – and back again.

Journey to Hades

However, for most Romans the journey to Hades was for ever. The souls of the dead were rowed across the mythical River Styx to Hades. A coin was placed in the dead person's mouth to pay the ferryman. With its connections with death and decay, Hades also gave the Romans an explanation for the dark months of winter.

 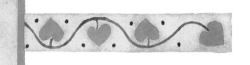

The goddess and the pomegranate

This Roman myth tells how Proserpina was kidnapped by Dis, king of the Underworld. The story is based on the Greek myth of Persephone (Proserpina) and Hades (Dis).

The goddess, Ceres, protector of plants and harvests, had a beautiful daughter called Proserpina. One day, Proserpina was picking flowers in the woods, when she suddenly noticed a bright narcissus, a rich, deep yellow like gold.

"I'll pick it for my mother," Proserpina decided. But as she bent down to pluck the flower, a great gaping hole opened up in the ground and from it emerged a terrible figure - Dis, king of the Underworld. He grabbed hold of Proserpina and dragged her down into the depths of the Earth.

Proserpina called out to Jupiter to help her, but the king of the gods was too far away and could not hear her cries. Her mother, Ceres, did hear her voice. For nine days and nights, she wandered the Earth, without food or sleep, trying to find her daughter. On the tenth day, she met the all seeing Sun god, who told her what had happened.

"Jupiter is the one you should blame," he told her. "For it was he who gave Dis permission to take Proserpina as his wife."

Ceres was so filled with grief at her daughter's loss, and so furious at Jupiter's treachery, that she neglected the plants she usually cared for, so that harvests failed and everything on Earth withered and died. Then, disguised as a frail old woman, she began her long, long search to find her daughter. Meanwhile, the gods were worried. Unless the crops grew, the whole world would starve. So, one by one, they went to Ceres and begged her to change her mind

"No," replied Ceres. "I will not let the crops grow until I see my daughter again."

There was nothing else for it, Jupiter had to give in. He sent his messenger, Mercury, to the Underworld to bring Proserpina back.

"But," he warned. "If she has eaten anything from Dis's garden, she is doomed to stay in Hades forever."

Proserpina returned from the Underworld and her mother was filled with joy. But when Ceres asked Proserpina if she had eaten Dis's food, her joy quickly turned to sorrow.

"I only ate some pomegranate," Proserpina said. "Surely that can't do any harm."

But it could. For pomegranates were a symbol of marriage. Ceres begged Jupiter not to take her daughter away again. And Jupiter, mindful that the Earth was still dying, acted kindly.

"You will spend part of the year in Hades with Dis," he decreed. "And the rest on Earth with your mother."

And this is why the Earth has seasons. While Proserpina stays in the Underworld with her husband, Ceres mourns, the plants and crops die, and the world has winter. When Proserpina returns to Earth, Ceres is happy again. The plants begin to bloom and blossom again, and it is spring.

Secret Caves

Carved out from hillsides by water and weathering, caves provided early people with their homes and perhaps their first temples, where they painted magical pictures of the animals they hunted. Caves could be secret and mysterious, too. Some were said to shelter mythical beasts. Others were secret hiding places away from the rest of the world – refuges for hermits or even the king of the gods.

Spirit Shelters

The real-life homes of bears and other animals, caves were often thought to house mythical creatures, from fire-breathing dragons to mischievous spirits. The Native Americans of the north-west coast of North America believed that such Earth spirits lived in caves in the cliffs which lined the seashore. From time to time, the spirits crept out to steal fishing gear or to play other tricks on the fishermen.

Hermit's Home

Often in remote places, some caves provided shelter for holy men and hermits. In the 2nd century AD, the Christian saint, Paul the Hermit, spent most of his life living in a cave in the Egyptian desert. Here he could pray and meditate, hidden from his Roman persecutors. Each day a raven brought him half a loaf of bread to eat. When another hermit came to visit, the raven brought a whole loaf!

Birthplace of Zeus

At 2,456 metres, Mount Ida, the "high one", is the highest mountain on the island of Crete, in the Mediterranean. In its side was a sacred cave which the Ancient Greeks believed to be the birthplace of Zeus, king of the gods. Many pilgrims visited the cave, among them Pythagoras, the famous mathematician. Archaeologists have found many ancient offerings there, including statues and cauldrons, a bronze shield and a drum.

This statue of Zeus dates from the 4th century BC.

The birth of Zeus

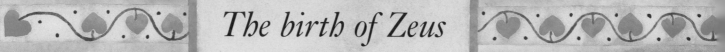

This is the story of how Zeus was born in a cave on Mount Ida.

◆

Long ago, a mighty giant, Kronos, King of the Titans, ruled the Earth. He married the goddess, Rhea, and had three daughters and three sons. But Kronos had been given a terrible warning – one of his children would one day destroy him and seize his throne. To make sure that this never happened, he swallowed each baby as it was born.

Rhea, his wife, was filled with grief and despair. How could she save her children? When the time drew near for the birth of her sixth child, she fled to Crete and hid in a deep cave on the mountainside. There the baby was born. Rhea called him Zeus.

But the danger was not yet over. Leaving her son for safe-keeping with two gentle nymphs, Rhea returned to Kronos. "Give me the child," demanded her husband. And Rhea wrapped a large stone in a blanket, to look like a baby, and gave it to Kronos, who happily swallowed it whole.

Thanks to his mother's quick thinking, Zeus grew up without his father knowing anything of his existence.

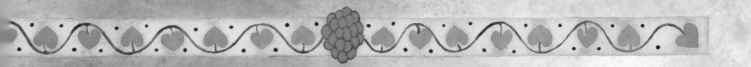

The nymphs brought up the young god with great love and care. They rocked him in a golden cradle and gave him goat's milk to drink. Spirits called the Curetes stood guard outside the cave, clashing their weapons whenever the baby cried, to hide the sound from his hot-tempered father. As soon as Zeus grew up, he vowed to punish his wicked father. But he could not decide what best to do so he asked Metis, the beautiful goddess of wisdom, for help. Metis had a clever plan. She made her way to Kronos's palace and slipped a powerful potion into his drink – and Kronos began to cough. He coughed and coughed until he brought up all of Zeus's brothers and sisters, swallowed so many years before. He even coughed up Rhea's great stone. Now mighty Zeus appeared and banished his father to the ends of the Earth where a hundred-armed giant stood guard. Then Zeus became king of the gods, ruling the Earth in his father's place, with his brothers and sisters beside him.

Fountains of Fire

Deep beneath the Earth lies a layer of red-hot, liquid rock. When gas builds up underground, it pushes the rock upwards, until it bursts to the surface, in a cloud of ash, smoke and steam – a volcano is erupting. The molten rock floods down the volcano's sides in glowing rivers. No one can be sure how far they will stretch.

Workshop of the Gods

An erupting volcano is one of the most awesome and terrifying sights in nature. Before their true cause was understood, most people believed that the explosions were the work of angry gods. Indeed, volcanoes are named after the Roman god, Vulcan, blacksmith to the gods and god of fire. He had his workshop inside the Solfatara volcano, near Naples, Italy. The rumbling sound that came from the volcano was said to be Vulcan hammering away at his forge.

Hawaiian Volcanoes

The islands which make up
Hawaii are the tops of huge,
underwater volcanoes which have
bubbled up over millions of years and
are still bubbling! Between 1843-1984,
the volcano Mauna Loa erupted about once
every four and a half years. But Kilauea is the world's
most active volcano. It has erupted non-stop since 1983.

A Goddess's Anger

According to legend, Kilauea is the home of the fiery
goddess, Pele, the creator of Hawaii. She is said to live
deep inside the volcano's crater. When she is angry, she
stamps her feet and makes the volcano erupt. In
ancient times, people built temples to Pele on
the volcano's slopes and threw offerings
of food, drink and flowers into the
crater to keep her happy. Just before an
eruption Pele was said to appear, disguised
as an old woman. Other people claimed
to see her face in the clouds.

*A wooden
carving
of Pele*

This is the story of how the goddess, Pele, came to live in Kilauea.

Some people say that the goddess, Pele, came from the island of Tahiti. She longed to travel and, one day, tucking her sister under her arm, she set off in a great, carved canoe. With her went a whole host of gods, to steer the canoe over the ocean.

So Pele travelled from island to island, looking for a place to live. Wherever she landed, lightning flashed, thunder rumbled and raged, and red-hot tongues of lava sped across the ground. But Pele could not find a home. Whenever she dug a hole in the ground, the sea rolled in and drove her away. At last, she dug a deep, deep hole in the great volcano of Kilauea. It was solid rock all the way down. And there Pele stayed.

Although Pele was beautiful, she was very hot-tempered. She only had to stamp her foot and a volcano erupted somewhere nearby. Woe betide anyone who made her angry. This did not stop Kamapua'a, the Pig-man, from falling madly in love with her. Kamapua'a had the power to turn himself into a pig. When he appeared as a human, he wore a long cloak to hide the bristles on his back. Pele could not stand the sight of him. "Go away and leave me alone," she shrieked. "I don't want to marry a pig. Even if you were the last pig alive."

Their quarrels grew worse and worse. Pele covered the Pig-man in showers of flames. He, in turn, put out her fires with fog and rain, and overran her home with pigs. Soon all the fires on Hawaii went out and the islands were plunged into darkness. It was time for the gods to act, and quickly. To keep Pele and the Pig-man apart, the gods divided the islands of Hawaii between the two of them. The places where the lava flowed belonged to Pele; the places where it always rained to the Pig-man. And so fire returned to Hawaii, bursting up from the ground and lighting up the sky whenever the goddess is angry.

The Shaking Earth

The Earth's crust is not a solid sphere of rock. It is cracked into gigantic pieces called plates, which rest on the layer of softer rock beneath. The plates are constantly pushed and jostled together, putting the rocks of the crust under great strain. All of a sudden, the ground can give way with a mighty crack. This is an earthquake. Some earthquakes are hardly felt. Others can reduce whole cities to rubble.

Early Beliefs

The mysterious quaking of the Earth baffled ancient people. Could it be caused by a gigantic animal? Some blamed the burrowing of a giant mole. Others blamed fish. One African myth tells of a huge fish which carried a stone on its back. The stone supported a cow which balanced the world on its horns. Earthquakes happened as the cow juggled the world from horn to horn. The Japanese, too, believed a fish was the cause of earthquakes.

How a giant catfish shook the world

This story comes from Japan where there are many powerful earthquakes.

◆

People dreaded the time of year when the gods left Earth to return to heaven, for then the ground began to tremble and shake. Great cracks opened up beneath people's feet, swallowing up houses, fields and villages.

"We must ask the gods to save us," the people said. They prayed to the gods, and left gifts of flowers at their shrines, until the gods agreed to help. But first they had to find out what was making the Earth shake.

The gods searched high and low – on the tops of mountains, under the sea, and even in heaven itself. Then they looked deep beneath the Earth, where they found a gigantic catfish. Normally, the fish slept, lying quite still in its underground home. But sometimes it grew restless. It wriggled and writhed, and flapped its tail, and this is what made the ground shake. The gods picked up an enormous stone and placed it right on top of the catfish, so it could not move an inch. "And that's the end of that," they said, happily.

But it wasn't, quite. Every now and again, the catfish gives a great wriggle and pushes the stone away. And then the ground trembles and shakes, and great cracks open up beneath people's feet, until the gods replace the stone.

Andvari's gold

**This is the story of how Andvari the Dwarf's treasure
was stolen by the god of mischief, Loki.**

Many years ago, three gods were on a visit to the land of humankind, dressed as ordinary men – Odin, father of the gods, Loki, god of mischief-making and Honir, the great warrior. As they strolled along a river bank, they spied an otter catching a salmon.

"We'll have that salmon for our supper," said Loki. He threw a stone which killed the otter. The fish was theirs. Loki cooked the salmon for his friends. Then he cut off the otter's fine skin to keep. That night the three men asked for shelter at a nearby farm. The farmer, Hreidmar, was gruff and rude, but he took the men in and soon they fell asleep. As soon as their eyes closed, Hreidmar's sons seized their guests and tied them up.

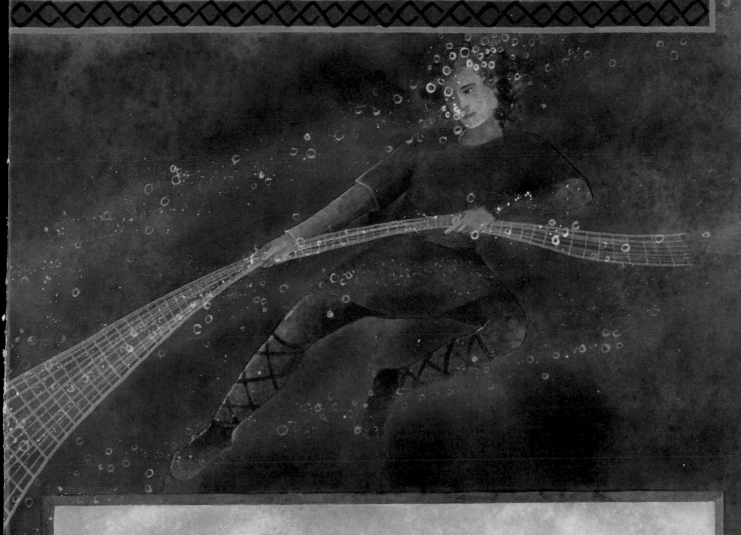

"I should kill you here and now," growled Hreidmar. "For that otter skin you carry belonged to my son. Every day, I turned him into an otter to go fishing. And you have killed him."

The gods were astonished. They offered to repay Hreidmar for what they had done, if only he would spare their lives. "Cover the otter skin with gold," he told them. "Then I will set you free."

Loki was sent to fetch the gold. He dived to the bottom of the sea to borrow the sea goddess's magic net which caught whatever you told it to. Then he found a deep, dark underground pool. He cast the net and caught a huge pike, which immediately turned into Andvari, the Dwarf, who could take the shape of a fish. Andvari was famous for his fabulous store of gold, which he kept well hidden from prying eyes. He was sure to have gold a-plenty for covering an otter skin.

"Unless you give me your gold," Loki threatened. "I shall keep you as my prisoner for ever. Which is it to be?"

Andvari had no choice. In fear of his life, he led Loki to his secret store and helped him fill his sack with gold. Just as he was about to leave, Loki spotted Andvari's golden ring and demanded it from him.

"Take it," said Andvari. "But be warned. Whoever wears that ring is cursed. The ring will destroy its wearer."

But Loki was not listening. He took the gold and returned to Hreidmar who, true to his word, set Odin and Honir free. The otter skin was covered in gold, from head to tail apart from one last whisker. The only gold left was Andvari's ring, which Loki handed over, making no mention of the curse that went with it.

It was not long before Hreidmar's family began to fall out over the gold. Greedy to get his hands on it, Hreidmar's son, Fafnir, murdered his father and ran away with the gold so he did not have to share it with his brother. He buried it away deep underground, and turned into a dragon to guard it. Was the curse of the ring at work?

It seemed it was, for Hreidmar's sons and grandsons fought and killed each other for the gold over the years to come until none of the men in the family was left alive. As the Dwarf himself had foretold, Andvari's gold brought nothing but misery to those who owned it.

Notes and Explanations

Who's Who

ANCIENT GREEKS: The people who lived in Greece from about 2,000BC. They worshipped many gods and goddesses who controlled the natural world and daily life.

ANCIENT ROMANS: The people who lived in Italy from about 750BC to AD476, named after the ancient city of Rome, founded in about 753BC. By 100BC, the Romans ruled over a huge empire centred around the Mediterranean Sea.

CELTS: A warrior-like people who first lived in Austria and France from about 600BC. Celtic tribes gradually spread across southern and western Europe, travelling over the sea to Britain and Ireland. The Celts were famous for their beautiful jewellery, music and poetry which told the stories of their gods and heroes.

CHRISTIANS: Followers of Jesus Christ, a teacher and preacher who lived 2,000 years ago in Palestine. Christians believe he is the Son of God. Today, there are about 200 million Christians, all over the world.

INCAS: The people who lived in the Andes mountains of South America. At the beginning of the 16th century, they ruled over an empire which covered much of modern-day Peru, Ecuador, Bolivia and Chile. By 1533, they themselves had been conquered by Spanish invaders.

PYTHAGORAS: A Greek mathematician and philosopher who was born in about 580BC. Pythagoras is most famous for his work in geometry. Many of his ideas are still used today, including his famous theorem on right-angled triangles.

VIKINGS: The Vikings were a sea-faring people from Scandinavia who raided and conquered many parts of northern Europe between the 8th and 11th centuries AD.

VIRGIL: A Roman poet who lived from 70-19BC. His most famous work is called *The Aeneid*, a long poem which tells the story of the origin and growth of the Roman Empire. Its hero is a prince, called Aeneas who was the ancestor of Romulus and Remus, the legendary founders of Rome.

What's What

Strictly speaking, fables, legends and myths are all slightly different. But the three terms are often used to mean the same thing – a symbolic story or a story with a message.

FABLE: A short story, not based on fact, which often has animals as its central characters and a strong moral lesson to teach.

LEGEND: An ancient, traditional story based on supposed historical figures or events. Many legends are based on myths.

MYTH: A story which is not based in historical fact but which uses supernatural characters to explain natural phenomena, such as the weather, night and day and so on.

IMMORTALITY: Immortality means living for ever, never dying or aging. In many religions, the gods were believed to be immortal.

ORACLE: A sacred place where people went to consult a god or goddess. Oracle also means the priest or priestess who spoke to people on the god's behalf.

PILGRIMS: People who make a special journey, or pilgrimage, to a sacred place as an act of religious faith and devotion. Sacred places include natural sites, such as rivers and mountains, and places connected with events in the history of a religion.

PLATES: The Earth's crust is not a solid sheet of rock. It is cracked into huge pieces, called plates. These float on a layer of soft rock beneath. As the plates collide or jerk away from each other, they cause earthquakes and volcanoes.

SOUL: The inner part or spirit of a person or animal, as opposed to its physical body. Many people believe the soul gives life to the body and, unlike the body, it never dies.

SULPHUR: Sulphur is a strong-smelling gas which is given off when a volcano erupts. It smells like rotten eggs.

Where's Where
The map below shows where in the world the places named in this book are found.

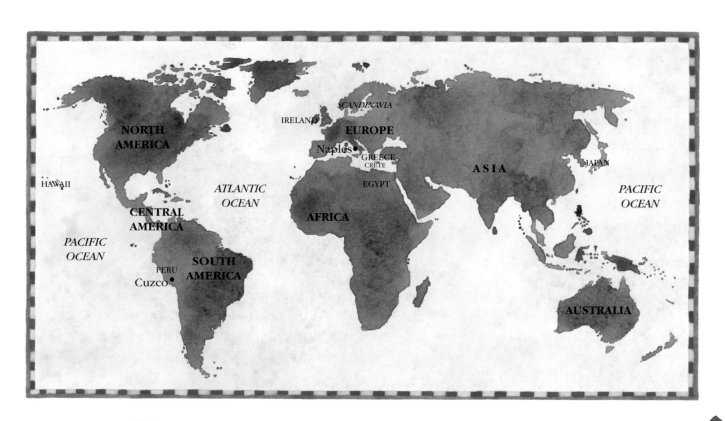